THUNDERSLEY
Postcard Memories

General FRANK L. DAVILL Stores.   TEAS.   NEWSAGENT.

THUNDERSLEY

Postcard Memories

Robert Delderfield
& David Hurrell

The Hadleigh & Thundersley
COMMUNITY ARCHIVE

DEDICATION

*In memory of our esteemed H&TCA colleague Val Jackson 1941 – 2018
and local historians, everywhere, who fly the flag for their community*

First published in 2019 by
Hadleigh & Thundersley Community Archive
Hadleigh Old Fire Station
Hadleigh, Benfleet
Essex SS7 2PA

E-mail: hadleighhistory@gmail.com
www.hadleighhistory.org.uk

As it has proven difficult to identify all possible remaining owners of copyright, if anyone believes (s)he owns the copyright of any of the images used in this book, we would be delighted to hear from you with a view to acknowledging this in any future printings.

Copyright © 2019 H&TCA

ISBN 978-0-9575958-5-9

All rights reserved. No part of this publication may be reproduced, stored in a retrieval system or transmitted in any form or by any means, electronic, mechanical, photocopying, recording or otherwise without prior permission from the publisher.

British Library Cataloguing in Publication Data
A catalogue record for this book is available from the British Library

Production: Graham Cook
Colour Origination and Design: David Hurrell

Printed in Spain

CONTENTS

Foreword   6

Acknowledgements   7
Dating and Condition Issues

Prologue: The Scattered Village   8

Tour One   9

Starting from the White Hart and along Kenneth Road, down Bread & Cheese Hill to Tarpots Corner then cirling right, along Rushbottom Lane, up Church Hill, past St Peter's Church and back towards the old village.

Tour Two   59

From the White Hart, exploring the Common – working towards Kingsley Lane and the Weir, back up Rayleigh Road to the Woodmans, west along Hart Road to Swans Green, up Dark Lane past the School and return to the White Hart.

Tour Three   83

Starting from the Woodmans Arms heading south along the Rayleigh Road to Victoria House Corner then west, as far as the Bread & Cheese.

Tour Four   98

Commencing again from the Woodmans junction we head east to the hamlet of Daws Heath, investigate the "Triangle" and continue to the extremity of Thundersley's parish by way of Bramble Road. On the return leg the woodlands are worthy of exploration.

Your Own Local History   106
An Armchair Tour

Multi-view cards, mystery items and misfits

Appendix   112

A brief history of postcards in Britain and clues to identifying their age

Map of Thundersley & Daws Heath   **Inside covers**

FOREWORD

This is the Hadleigh & Thundersley Community Archive's second book of postcard views and a companion to Robert Nichols' celebrated Hadleigh Postcard Memories. The images in this book were nearly all created during the first half of the 20th Century and, reproduced together as one volume, represent the most complete record ever created of the changes that have taken place in Thundersley, travelling back a little beyond the extremes of living memory.

H&TCA is one of six on-line archives formed early in 2010 as a joint initiative of Essex Record Office and Essex Libraries, with the financial support of the Heritage Lottery Fund. Tilbury and Chadwell have since joined the group; the pilot archive on Canvey also continues to prosper.

Each archive supports itself with events and, in our case, production of uniquely valuable books, authoritative research with professional scanning and restoration of postcards and other material showing how this area has looked, and thus how it is developing.

We carry out drop-in sessions, pop-up events in Thundersley, Daws Heath and Hadleigh, maintaining an office at Hadleigh Old Fire Station – Hadleigh's landmark community hub.

We are delighted that so many people continue to give unfailing support, coming to organised events, contributing personal histories in text, historic documents and pictures to the website at www.hadleighhistory.org.uk and buying our books, of course! Some contributors, commentators and purchasers represent the diaspora of people emigrated one, two or more generations ago from around here and now live in France, Canada, the USA, Australia, New Zealand and elsewhere.

Many of us have experience of the careful curating of the historic built environment in countries like Italy and Austria. Comparison with the apparently casual and relentless destruction of old properties and historic assets in our corner of southeast Essex is all the more striking. Residents can appreciate the importance of documenting Thundersley and Hadleigh's constantly changing appearance. With their help, we enable previously unseen historic documents, pictures and postcards, to remain accessible for present and future generations by publishing them on our website and in books like this one.

The residents of Thundersley have oft said, "Where is *our* Postcard book, the companion work to Hadleigh Postcard Memories which showcased Mr Nichols unique collection of postcards and personal commentary?" Well, here it is – and may it bring much delight!

The Editorial Board
Hadleigh & Thundersley Community Archive

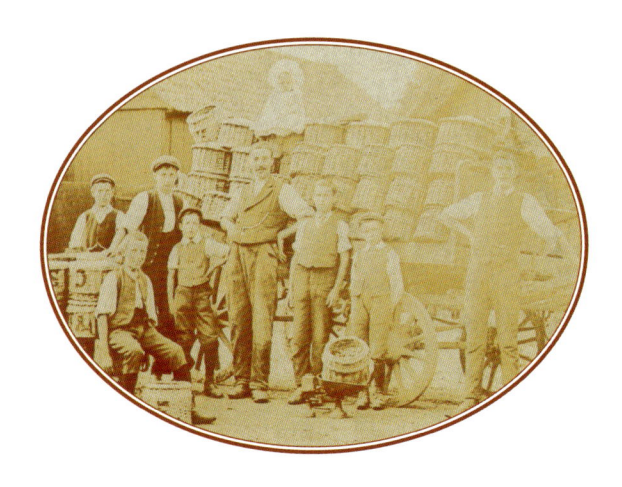

ACKNOWLEDGMENTS

Creating this book has been a labour of love: it is hoped that our efforts will evoke pleasant nostalgia for our very oldest viewers and interest and enlightenment for our youngest (who will doubtless be awestruck by the amazing changes that have occurred within the space of a mere century). The gathering of these images has been made uniquely possible by the dedication of the Hadleigh & Thundersley Community Archive's team of stalwart volunteers. Their immense contribution to the well-being of their community and their nurturing of civic pride is praiseworthy: to be a part of their team is both a joy and a privilege.

Much goodwill has been evident in the making of this book. Several people and institutions granted us access to their collections and we would like to record our thanks here as a lasting tribute.

A number of these postcards were scanned from the late Robert Nichols' private collection, with his agreement before his death in 2018 at the grand age of 97.

Many others came courtesy of the late Hewson Osborne's family (whose generosity provided the impetus for another of H&TCA's Heritage Lottery Fund projects).

The very much-missed Lynn Tait was something of an "institution" in the Leigh and Southend area. With her extraordinary vision, enthusiasm, energy and creative drive she did perhaps more than any other person in history, to promote the well-being of Leigh-on-Sea – certainly more than any politician ever could. Just a year after her death her family generously gave us access to Lynn's legendary postcard collection which, at a fairly late stage, caused (to our great delight) this book to be rather bigger than was intended. Lynn's Mother had been brought up in Benfleet and Thundersley, so understandably there were some "gems" in the box!

Peter Lewsey of Thundersley is a great friend of the Archive and gives us unlimited access to his collection of postcards.

Images have come from Peter Lewsey (64), Lynn Tait (54), Hewson Osborne (33), Robert Nichols (19), Gwyneth Craze (16), John Downer (13), Southend-on-Sea Museums Services (12), Bob Delderfield (7), Diane Ward (6), Eddie Curtis (5), Rita Brown (4), Gwyn Jordan (1), Jonathan Stamp (2), Richard Hills (2), Ernest Brooks (1) and Hadleigh & Thundersley Cricket Club (1).

We came across a goodly number of duplicates in the process of building our collection, but not so many as to undermine our certain confidence that many more images are still "out there" waiting to be collected! Where we had "swops", we simply scanned everything, chose the best example for printing and recorded the earliest postmark.

Finally, we had a lot of cards that didn't make the final edit. There are only so many versions of "St Peter's Church, Thundersley" or "View from the Churchyard" that one can stomach at one sitting.

Robert Delderfield & David Hurrell

DATING AND CONDITION ISSUES

It is not an easy matter to apply an accurate date for a postcard view. Postmarks, stamps and messages can be a guide but this only gives a last possible date: some of the images may date from considerably earlier (see Guide on page 112). Nevertheless, approximate and "last possible" dates have been recorded whenever possible, for interest's sake.

Many of the postcards had faded badly and oft-times the substrate itself had oxidised to a nicotine brown. Every image has been painstakingly computer-restored in order to bring out as much of the historical detail as possible – sometimes clearer than the original. However, the retoucher has strived to retain something of the character of the original card, for aesthetic reasons. Such a book as this is *never* a commercially sound enterprise, yet no expense has been spared in its production and 4-colour lithography has been used throughout.

PROLOGUE: THE SCATTERED VILLAGE

In the 19th and early 20th centuries Thundersley was a thinly sprawled parish, dispersed from east to west into several small centres of population in between which the farming of fields and woodlands took place. It is mainly since the 1930s, as farming in the village declined, that the gaps between these centres filled up with ever increasing speed.

The old manor house stood almost alone in the middle of its farmland which was spread across what we now call New Thundersley i.e. the flatland between Church Hill and Rushbottom Lane. St Peter's standing in its commanding position was linked to the village "centre" with a scattering of houses along Church Road. Today the term "village" as used by Thundersley residents tends to refer to the shops and houses around the White Hart and the primary school.

Another area of shops and houses had grown up along the Rayleigh Road especially close to the Woodmans Arms. This was understandable because it was the traditional main road via Rayleigh Market to London from Hadleigh and Leigh. A new small residential area had sprung up from the 1790s onwards at Daws Heath. The development of this hamlet was a slow process with short bursts especially in the 1930s and 1970s. On Thundersley's southern edge, Kiln Road and London Road always had a sprinkling of cottages but began to develop seriously with the arrival of motor cars, charabancs and the attractions of Southend, particularly after the First World War.

This rather untidy development of Thundersley parish created a problem for us of how to arrange 200 postcards in some logical order. We chose eventually to display them as four "virtual" tours of Thundersley. They may be physically "walked" though they vary considerably in length. Those who choose to walk may be amused – and even encouraged (as we ourselves were) – that we conspired to start and finish near pubs!

Chronology is, of necessity, completely ignored, so our readers will find themselves leaping to and fro between decades as if conveyed by a Tardis! A map on the inner covers shows the routes and coloured spots indicate the locations (as best as we can gauge).

This is the reverse of the postcard opposite.

TOUR ONE

TOUR ONE (3.8 miles) is rather long and very hilly and, if walking, might best be tackled in bite-sized sections. It starts conveniently at the old village's central watering hole, the White Hart, beside the smithy and wheelwrights. Just beyond the public house we pass the quaint old terrace known as Hart Cottages to our left and then proceed westwards along the old Church Rd (renamed as Hart Rd). To our right is the imposing Raymonds Farmhouse, behind the village pond. Our journey to the T-junction we can see ahead of us is interrupted briefly by a diversion into Raymonds Drive to view the houses that have replaced the farm's fields. Back on Church Road again we arrive at the junction with Kenneth Road known locally as Pond's Corner, named after the family that ran the nearby shop.

We now follow Kenneth Road and walk this leafy lane for a half mile or so until it meets the Kiln Road. En route we are able to admire some of the splendid and recently built houses and, towards the end of the road, on our right, the Congregational Church. We emerge where Kiln Road meets Bread and Cheese Hill and heads west towards the Capital (as do we) but it is only just becoming a favoured route for commercial traffic, which historically went via Rayleigh, Wickford, Billericay and Brentwood. For horse-drawn traffic Bread & Cheese Hill is as dangerous going down as it is tiring coming up, and in places is barely even wide enough for carts to pass. The River Thames is only a mile and a half to our left and can be glimpsed if we detour briefly to admire Jarvis Hall or to stand atop the Devil's Steps. Descending the wooded coombe we enter a built-up area approaching Tarpots crossroads, where the London Road (High Road) heads off towards South Benfleet and the Canvey Island ferry. We head up Rushbottom Lane and bear right up Church Road, into an area of good flat arable land which very slowly developed from the 1890s onwards into an urban sprawl known as "New" Thundersley. Plenty to see and admire here, including the old Manor House and its farm, a picturesque pond and distant brickworks. The spire of the diminutive 12th Century Church dedicated to St Peter (but once St Michael's) is visible atop the eminence of the Thundersley escarpment, occasionally hidden behind statuesque elms. The strenuous climb up is amply rewarded by extraordinary views towards London and across the Crouch plain to Wickford and beyond. The remainder of our journey along Church Road passes some interesting businesses and the Old Church School before we arrive back at the starting point of this tour.

1 Blacksmith's, postmarked 1907
The blacksmith's shop stood next to the White Hart Inn. It was not uncommon for a hostelry to have a smithy very close by, but at least two of the licensees of the White Hart combined the jobs of publican and blacksmith.

2 The White Hart Inn, postmarked 1952
Post World War II, all is quiet in the village, except for a small group of men chatting in front of the White Hart. The row of shops on the right has little changed today but now there are plenty of shops on the left just beyond the pub. Spot the pillar box and the phone booth.

3 The White Hart Inn
There seems to be a queue outside the old smithy in this well-peopled village scene of the 1930s. Everyone by then would have been used to a brick-faced White Hart with a rough-cast rear. The old wooden exterior began to disappear in the first decade of the twentieth century.

4 Hart Cottages
Just south of the White Hart these lovely old cottages stood at the bend in Hart Road. The building was once called The Horse Shoes which had been, it would seem, the village pub before the White Hart opened around 1797. The cottages were replaced by a row of four shops, built by Wiggins, in 1961.

White Hart Corner, Thundersley. 8.

5 White Hart Cottages, postmarked 1919
Another view of the old cottages but to the right of them are the white fence and gate that once led into Dark Lane. The other white fence on the immediate left acted as a guard to prevent people and vehicles from accidentally slipping into the village pond especially at night.

64336. THUNDERSLEY.

6 Thundersley Village Pond
In a wider shot of the same scene as the previous post card the photographer is standing at the entrance to Raymonds Farm which lay to the immediate left. Whilst refreshing themselves in the White Hart, carters would often leave their vehicles in the pond to swell the wooden felloes in the wheels.

7 Hart Road circa 1955
Chatsworth, the house with the turret, was built by Cyril Wiggins for his family in 1932. In 2001 it was sold along with the next door bungalow for £460,000, demolished and replaced by flats. A much earlier demolition took place when the first house on the left became the village car park.

8 Raymonds Farm, circa 1912
Raymonds' 170 acres of farmland once extended along Church Road as far as St Peter's to the west and to Thundersley Common and Great Burches Road to the north. For a short period during Stephen Harvey's tenure in the late 19th century it was sometimes also known as Raylands.

9 Raymonds Farm, postmarked 1907
In the foreground is the village pond and partially hidden behind bushes is the farmhouse, which in 1924 became the headquarters of Wiggins the builders. Godden Lodge now stands at this point in Hart Road.
[See article Changing Face of Thundersley Village in www.hadleighhistory.org.uk]

10 Church Road (now Hart Road)
The road between Dark Lane and Kenneth Road was once part of Church Road. In this wonderfully rural scene we would today be standing just west of Avington Walk and looking west towards Pond's Corner. The houses glimpsed in the trees on the left are still there today, unlike Raymonds' field on the right.

11 Church Road (now Hart Road)
We are still looking west as in the previous postcard but somewhat later and now nearer Kenneth Road. The Type B Omnibus provides us with a post 1910 date. Digby's stores on the right has had many guises over the years, including ironmonger and barber.
[See also postcard 97]

12 Raymonds Drive
This is Raymonds Drive as it looked in the late 1920s. The photographer is looking south with Grandview Drive on his immediate left. Uplands, the first house on the left and most of the other neighbouring houses are still there today.

13 Raymonds Drive
The houses and bungalows seen here are in the middle of Raymonds Drive. All the houses on the right are there today although many of them have, not surprisingly, over some 90 years or more, been heavily altered and modernised.

14 Kenneth Road
Whitehaven and Stanley House, the two houses on the left, stand prominently at the north end of Kenneth Road not far from the mini-roundabout. Stoneleighs now divides Stanley House from the smaller house seen under the tree canopy. This third house no longer has a chimney.

15 Kenneth Road
With Coombewood Drive on our left, the bungalows seen on the right have now been altered in appearance, some considerably. Today Kenneth Road is very busy with traffic in contrast to the leafy quietness revealed in all six of the postcards shown in this book.

16 Kenneth Road, postmarked 1941
We are now facing south and nearer to the London Road where the road still has a mild double bend. The photographer is standing beside 123 Kenneth Road.

17 Southern end of Kenneth Road
In the distance is Kiln Road (A13) where nowadays we are used to seeing Hobson's military uniform factory on the left at the junction. The photographer's viewpoint is probably taken beside Kingsland House which still stands, on the corner of Bradley Avenue. The thin white traffic warning sign tells us a school once stood just beyond it.

18 Thundersley Congregational Church
Congregationalism has been established on the corner of Kenneth Road since 1906 but the old church pictured here has been replaced by a larger, modern church and hall to cope with its thriving community. It is now known as The Beacon. The land on which the church stands was once part of Coombe Wood and was originally intended as a site for an hotel.

19 Thundersley Congregational Church

The distinctive bell-tower of the Congregational Church stands out behind the young lady. On the far left can be seen part of a building, once The Manse, which in 1929 became the council offices of the new Benfleet District Council. (Prior to that Rochford Rural District Council had control of the area.)

20 Retreat Refreshment Rooms, Bread & Cheese Hill

The Retreat stood on Kiln Road almost opposite Kenneth Road. This is a particularly splendid and typical Edwardian scene with ladies in their long skirts and summer blouses and a couple of boy scouts in uniform.

21 View from the Devil's Steps
To reach the 44 steep steps these days one is obliged to pick up the footpath leading from Mount Crescent. This well tramped path was always the most direct (albeit treacherous) pedestrian route from South Benfleet to Thundersley. The view depicted here is nowadays completely hidden by tree growth.

22 Bread & Cheese Hill, postmarked 1912
Here's a glimpse, near the top of Bread & Cheese Hill, of when the road was narrow and bushes encroached on both sides.

23 Bread & Cheese Hill, postmarked 1905
In another very early postcard of the hill, about 1905, we have moved a short distance downwards. Thundersley Park Road is bearing off to the left with its famous shop, at various times a general stores and/or a café. How hikers and cyclists would have appreciated a café after toiling up the hill!

24 The Cyclists' Rest, London Road, postmarked 1905
Here is a rare side view of what was then the Cyclists' Rest, a name also used at a different period by Packham's further down Bread & Cheese Hill. This is the same building as that shown in postcards 22 and 23. Although recently pulled down and the site re-developed, it appeared in many postcards over the years.

25 Coombe Wood, postmarked 1914
Coombe Wood lies behind the house on the north side of Bread and Cheese Hill. The rather grand residence was built before the 1st World War but is no longer with us. It stood a short way down the hill just below where Thundersley Park Road emerges on the other side of the road.

26 Bread & Cheese Hill
Some road widening has taken place in the next three postcards for although the road seems deserted we are now into the age of the motor car. By the late twenties and the thirties summer brought thousands of visitors to the Southend district in charabancs, motor cars and on bicycles.

27 Bread & Cheese Hill
The hill, probably in the 1930s, gives us an almost entirely rural scene to view. Widening the road together with some landscaping of the verge has expanded the view for those descending the hill. Note also the proliferation of telegraph poles.

28 Bread & Cheese Hill
The motorbus begins its climb and is passing a cyclist who already has decided to walk up the hill. In the early 1900s and later the hill had its fair share of cycle accidents reported by the press. Especially dangerous it would seem was the downward journey.

29 Bread & Cheese Hill, postmarked 1910
   This view of the hill gives us a glimpse of Lodge House alias Packham's Stores in 1910 or earlier when the business, conducted then by Eliza Packham, was relatively quiet but developing. The family eventually ran not only a shop but also tea rooms and later still a long-surviving garage.

30 Packhams Refreshment Rooms, Bread & Cheese Hill, postmarked 1913
   It is now two or three years later than the previous postcard, with livelier advertising. At various times the house was called the Wheelers' Rest and the Cyclists' Rest because the London Road like its cousin, the Arterial Road, was particularly popular with cyclists in the inter-war years.

View from Bread & Cheese Hill, Thundersley.

31 View from Bread & Cheese Hill
The view here is taken from the summit of Thundersley Park Road. On the skyline the South Benfleet water tower can be seen. The large house on the left is Crescent House. It still stands in Mount Crescent and the current owner has given it a considerable face-lift. The Devil's Steps drop away through the trees to the right.

Jarvis Hall. BENFLEET.

32 Jarvis Hall Farm
The extensive but dilapidated hall farm buildings are neatly framed by the greenery. The hall itself is in the far background partly hidden by the tree on the right. Look for the chimney.

JARVIS HALL, BENFLEET. 1930.

33 Jarvis Hall
Although the house retains some evidence of its origins around 1400 and is a Grade II Listed building, it has succumbed to many alterations and additions over the centuries especially in the 17th and 19th centuries.

View Bread & Cheese Hill with King John's Hunting Lodge.

34 Bread & Cheese Hill with King John's Hunting Lodge, postmarked 1912
With ancient royal parks in Hadleigh and Thundersley it is not surprising that two or three old local buildings have over the years been identified with Kings' hunting parties. The great barn shown here gathered a legend associated with visits by King John in the 13th century, hence the publisher's choice of title.

35 King Henry VIII's Hunting Box
This is another view of the barn shown in postcard 34. The postcard collector in this case has chosen to link it to Henry VIII which sounds perfectly reasonable but little evidence exists. Henry gave Hadleigh Castle to three of his wives successively as a dower but whether he sampled the local hunting boxes is not known.

36 King John's Hunting Lodge, postmarked 1913
Yet another view of the subject of postcards 34 and 35 gives us a much closer view of this great old relic. It was taken down quite recently, in a much worse state than appears here, and has been replaced with an elegant new house built using old bricks.

View from Jarvis Hill, Thundersley. 2229

37 View from Jarvis Hill

Unfortunately, not only is this card undated but the viewpoint has not been discovered. It is undoubtedly taken from somewhere near Jarvis Hall. The delightful rural view with its small pond in the foreground remains a mystery.

38 Estuary View from Jarvis Hill

The editors spent an interesting but ultimately fruitless morning trying to find this splendid view. Estate agents were and still are always keen to fit into their blurb phrases such as "Views of the Thames". It remains a very good selling point.

39 Thundersley Church from London Road (reproduced from glass negative)
A completely clear view, impossible today, demonstrates, before trees hid it, the once dominating position of St. Peter's. The photographer (Alfred John Padgett) is standing at the junction of Spencer Road with Thundersley Church Road which cuts diagonally across the rows of north-south roads towards the church.

40 The Argosy, London Road, circa 1929
The Argosy shop and tea rooms is nowadays a Malaysian restaurant and stands on the corner of St Clements Road. Once the Argosy had occupied a building further to the east *[see 41]*. On the reverse of this card is the Postal Union Congress stamp of 1929 *[shown on the title page]*. In 1911 the proprietor was Joseph Cox but here it is C. J. Fox.

LONDON RD. THUNDERSLEY. *3405.*

41 The Argosy, London Road (reproduced from glass negative)
The nearest building on the right was soon to be the Argosy Stores *[see postcard 40]*. Shields Clothing Recycling now occupies the last building on the right, formerly known as London House, but which at this time was an earlier location of Argosy Stores. In the central distance is the Kents Hill crossroads.

TARPOTS.

42 Tarpots
The large building on the left is the oldest part of the parade of shops on the South Benfleet side of the London Road at Tarpots. The nearest shop, belonging to John Abrahams, has petrol pumps at its front. The service road is hidden by the bushes but was once the original main road.

Great Tarpots, Tarpots Hall.

43   Tarpots Hall
Tarpots Hall, a multi-purpose public hall for this rapidly developing area of Thundersley and South Benfleet, was opened in 1929. It catered for dances, plays, boxing, whist drives, wedding receptions and many other activities. It was also the home of the South Benfleet ATC and was known to many as the ATC Hall.

Tarpots Corner, Thundersley.

44   Tarpots Corner, postmarked 1936
Here we can see the Thundersley side of the London Road, including Tarpots Hall. Clearly the number of shops on both sides of the road was increasing, not forgetting the two shops at the front of the Hall, one of which was Tarpots Bakery.

Great Tarpots, The Main Road

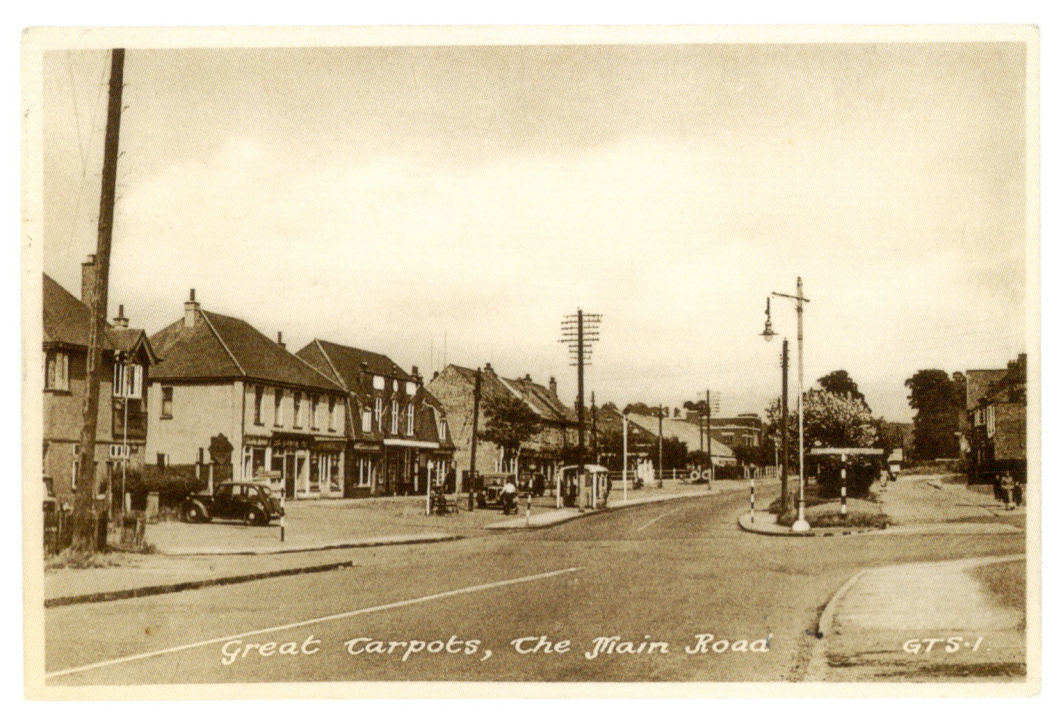

45 Cross Roads, Tarpots, postmarked 1956
Twenty years has gone by and the Hall has more company on the Thundersley side of the road with several new businesses between it and Rushbottom Lane. Both sides of the London Road have been provided with service roads.

Great Tarpots, The Corner.

46 Great Tarpots Corner
The focus here is on The Tarpot public house erected in 1933. Its first publican was Archibald "Archie" Wilson who remained the licensee until 1954 although by 1939 he had installed managers, Peter and Ada Thomson.

Cross Roads, Tarpots, Thundersley

47 Cross Roads, Tarpots
This postcard is a gem because it is not instantly recognised by most people. Believe it or not, from Rushbottom Lane we are looking across what we now call the A13 straight down Benfleet High Road. On the right close to the junction are buildings which were part of Great Tarpots Farm.

Great Tarbots Farm, Thundersley, near Pitsea.

48 Great Tarpots Farm
Together with its spelling error this early picture postcard shows Great Tarpots Farmhouse which stood on the western side of South Benfleet High Road a short distance from Tarpots crossroads.

49 The back of postcard 48, postmarked 1905
An unnamed "stony broke" writer sent this Xmas wish from Pitsea to an 11 year old Winifred, a solicitor's daughter. Although the card depicts a South Benfleet farm, the publisher's address is Pitsea. This can be seen by the small print in the left hand margin.

50 Great Tarpots Farm, postmarked 1920
Great Tarpots Farm's 166 acres spread into three parishes, South Benfleet, Thundersley and Bowers Gifford. The question arises: was there a Little Tarpots Farm? There certainly was. It stood on the south side of the London Road between St Clements and Gifford Roads.

51 Tarpots Pond (South Benfleet), postmarked 1927
This wintry scene shows one of two large ponds belonging to Great Tarpots Farm. As we can see, this pond lay alongside the Benfleet High Road, close to the farmhouse. The other pond was on the Thundersley side of the crossroads.

52 Tarpots Pond (Thundersley)
Here we see the second pond but in more summery conditions. It could once be found on the western corner of Rushbottom Lane and the London Road.

53 Rushbottom Lane, postmarked 1920

Formerly Rushey Bottom Lane or Watery Lane, this is one of the oldest byways of Thundersley. Once you could follow this peaceful route from Tarpots to North Benfleet village and on to Wickford. Driving down Rushbottom Lane today it is very hard to identify it with this rather romantic rural scene. However, north of the tunnel under the A130, walkers, cyclists and equestrians can still enjoy a similar tree-lined tranquility.

54 Church Road

The general stores in the right foreground later became a post office and stood at the Manor Road crossroads on the corner which is now occupied by the Zac Wilsher. On the left beside the first telegraph pole we can catch a glimpse of the Barn Steam Laundry.

55 Church Road, New Thundersley, postmarked 1913
The photographer, W. Sullivan of Hadleigh, was looking east, standing beside the shop in postcard 54. The first house on the right is still there. A group of people wandering along the unmade road appear to be mainly children. Nowadays Armstrong Road is on the left just past the building whose front you will see in the next postcard.

56 The Barn Steam Laundry
This imposing building has seen many changes. It still stands on the north side of Church Road between Manor Road and Armstrong Road. In 1911 the 20 year old laundry proprietor, Archibald Brooker, was employing a married couple in their thirties to manage the laundry. Archibald's father, John, was the owner of the Weybridge Laundry in Surrey.

57 The Old Manor House
Grade II Listed, the Manor House survives today although it is almost entirely hidden from view by houses in Manor Road and Church Road. The current building dates from about 1600. Before developments from the 1890s onward its 250 acre farm took up a large part of what we now call New Thundersley.

58 The Manor Pond, circa 1913
The Manor Farm pond was close beside Church Road and has been replaced by part of the Manor Industrial Estate. In the distance to the right of the two elm trees we can just see the Manor Brickworks which closed down in 1936. Some of the barns and outbuildings of the farm can be seen to the left.

59 The Manor Pond, circa 1913 (but postmarked 1926)
The same photographer, Alfred John Padgett of Station Road, Leigh-on-Sea, was responsible for these three pond cards, taken shortly before the 1st World War. Here he has swung his camera to the east, revealing more elms, a hay rick and three young people apparently deciding how to retrieve a football from the pond.

60 The Manor Pond, circa 1913
Our enthusiastic photographer has found yet another angle, pointing more south-easterly. Church Road is visible, running from centre right, and if you wish to see much more of the house that is sticking out to the left of the tree, go to the next postcard.

61 Church Road, New Thundersley
The house on the left is Hedingham House built in 1903 for his family by the manager of the Manor Brickworks, Edward Corder. It now stands on the corner of Hazlemere Road. All the bricks and tiles for the house were made at the nearby brickworks which flourished between the 1890s and 1936.

62 Kents Hill Road, New Thundersley (reproduced from glass negative)
Here are two of the earliest buildings in the Thundersley section of Kents Hill Road. The houses, which still stand today, also feature in postcard 82. The farther semi-detached stands on the corner of Chesterfield Avenue. The footpath looks narrow but firmly established. The road, however, is no more than a muddy track.

63 Thundersley Church from the road, postmarked 1913
The road is Church Road and the photo was taken somewhere near its junction with Stanley Road in about 1913. It is a view no longer available to us thanks to housing developments and trees. It is not easy now to spot St Peter's steeple whereas in the early days of New Thundersley it would have stood out.

64 Chesterfield Avenue, New Thundersley, postmarked 1921
This particular view both up to and down from the church was very popular with postcard publishers. Here we see Hillside House, one of the earliest residences in the road.

65 View of Thundersley Church from Chesterfield Avenue, postmarked 1936
In this slightly later view from Chesterfield another house, Hillside View, has been built and what was a green footpath has been cut and widened. Both houses remain today but much altered. Chesterfield was just one of very many roads which were developed in rural New Thundersley from the 1890s onwards.

66 The Church from New Thundersley, postmarked 1916
This huge green field with its footpath angled down to join Thundersley Church Road is no more. Very many years ago it was terraced to accommodate hundreds of graves of Thundersley villagers and is now enclosed within the churchyard.

67 Birds eye view, New Thundersley, postmarked 1912
From close to the foot of Church Hill we have a view across New Thundersley in about 1912 when it was still mainly farmland. The house we can see in Bassenthwaite Road was The Almonds and built in 1901. It survives today, re-named St Marys. One of the first to be erected in the "Lake District" it no longer has a "cat-slide" roof.

68 View from top of Church Road, circa 1913
Here we see a similar view but behind The Almonds we can see the first house in Keswick Road. Rather a grand home, and still with us, it was built in 1902 and called Keswick House. To the right is another pair of houses in Windermere Road. The left hand one, Lingford, survives and faces down Keswick Road.

69 Church Hill
This is the view that Malcolm Campbell (later Sir Malcolm Campbell) would have had as he neared the top of the Hill Climb (at 105 mph with two wheels off the ground according to Reverend Maley) in his Talbot car "Blue Bird" in 1920. To the right the rough road now gradually reduces to a wild path which takes a pedestrian through to Rhoda Road North.

70 St Peter's Church
This picture gives us an impression of the steep slope upon which much of the northern section of the graveyard lies. Today a combination of badger activity and the crumbly steepness of the hill has made the north west corner of the churchyard inaccessible.

71 St. Peter's Church, postmarked 1929

In this card of the late 1920s we have advanced from the bend in Church Hill into the churchyard and have a good view of the oldest part of St Peter's, rebuilt after a disastrous fire in 1215. The slightly lower roof at the eastern end of the building belongs to a later chancel built in 1880.

72 St Peter's Church Rectory

Built in the 1880s the Rectory, shown here in the 1920s, had to be replaced after structural weaknesses appeared. A large crack may be seen running down the low wall of the conservatory.

73 Lychgate, St Peter's
An inscription over the gate tells us it was erected in 1918 as a token of love and esteem by parishioners and friends of the late Rector, Revd. Thomas Noon Talfourd Major. Today it stands to one side of the current pathway having lost its original purpose to shelter a coffin or bier and the pall-bearers before a burial.

74 Lych Gate and Church
The path from gate to church door at this time took parishioners close to the east end of the building then turned sharp left past the east window and then right to the door.

75 St Peter's Church, circa 1906
Approaching St Peter's from the west, before the lych gate was added, we see to the left Church Cottage which at present (2019) is receiving major alterations and refurbishment.

76 St Peter's
The photographer has neatly aligned the two roofs of the church with that of the lych gate. The latter was built in the traditional style with the gate at one end of the roofed area and not in the middle as is the case with many more recent lych gates.

77 St Peter's
In this card, the church is shown as seen from the Rectory. It is interesting to note a low wall, now no longer in existence, dividing the Rectory grounds from the churchyard. The view also demonstrates clearly how small the original church was before the 1880 extension (on the right) was added.

78 Interior, St Peter's, c. 1911
We are standing in the oldest part of the church, before the 1st World War, looking towards the chancel and sanctuary of the Victorian extension. We are, however, able to see two of the hugely thick pillars, typical of Norman architecture, in the old church.

ST. PETER'S CHURCH, THUNDERSLEY

79 interior, St Peter's
Once again here is the interior of St Peter's before it was considerably expanded in 1966. Particularly noteworthy is the 13th century font in the right foreground.

VIEW FROM CHURCHYARD, THUNDERSLEY.

80 View from the churchyard
The next five views from St Peter's across the slowly developing New Thundersley are almost impossible to locate now owing to the growth of trees in the churchyard. This one looks in a south westerly direction. The next four gradually swing round until we are looking to the north west.

81 Across country from Thundersley Church (reproduced from glass negative)
If we look closely, Chesterfield Avenue is visible running alongside the right hand margin of the postcard. More than a fair sprinkling of New Thundersley plotland houses can be distinguished although the roads are mere tracks where often one end does not yet link comfortably with the other end.

82 New Thundersley from Church Hill
Stretching before us fairly centrally is Chesterfield Avenue in one of the earlier postcards. To the right stands Hillside House shown previously from the west in postcard 64. The two prominent pairs of semi-detached houses in the middle ground in a rudimentary Kents Hill Road are still there today. *[See postcard 62]*

83 View from Church Hill
Slightly later than the previous postcard, still looking down Chesterfield Avenue, we can see not only Hillside House but also Hillside View just beyond it. *[See postcard 65]* From the lack of buildings on view it is highly likely that both this card and the previous one date from well before the 1st World War.

84 View from Church Hill
Looking very lonely, Stanley House stands in Stanley Road but it no longer exists. The hedge line which appears just above the roof of Stanley House runs along Church Road. Long rows of now lost elm trees were common features on postcards of Thundesley. Note the bee hives, bottom left. *[See also article Stanley House in www.hadleighhistory.org.uk]*

85 View from Thundersley Church, postmarked 1948
Down on the flatlands below Church Hill, the plotland developments and their roads remained unmade and unadopted for many, many years. This view is now completely hidden by tree growth but it is possible to find some of the graves shown in the scene.

86 Church Road
This rather lovely view includes the old Tithe Barn, the first building on the left of the road. Next to it is Church Cottage and beyond we can see the spire of St Peter's. Sadly, in 1969 a mighty blaze destroyed the old barn.

ST PETER'S & RECTORY, THUNDERSLEY

87 St Peter's and Rectory
If you walk up Grasmere Road to where the houses end and drop down on to the footpath beyond you will find yourself near to the photographer's viewpoint. He must have stood on the slope of the private land to your right and looked across towards the church which today remains invisible, cloaked by trees.

VIEW FROM GRASMERE RD. THUNDERSLEY.   6299.

88 View from Grasmere Road
From the high northern end of Grasmere Road the footpath still exists and there is still a broad landscape to be seen extending out over the valley of the River Crouch.

89 Hand's Store, Church Road, postmarked 1908
This rare postcard, much restored, reveals that George W. Hand's store selling newspapers, confectionery and tobacco also served tea and refreshments. Today it is a convenience store and post office with the sorting office behind it.

90 Davill's General Stores, postmarked 1916
When Frank & Dorothy Davill lived here in the early 20th century the house was called Chestnut Cottage. The shop was a general store and newsagents and had previously been run by George Hand who had turned his mind and hand to market gardening.

Post Office Corner, Thundersley. T. 5.

91 Post Office, postmarked 1956
In this view at Pond's Corner we can see that the shop once run by the Hands and the Davills has a small extension at the rear and is now a post office. The main sorting office was yet to be built. Nowadays this once peaceful junction is busy with traffic all day long and has a mini-roundabout.

Church Schools, Thundersley. 7.

92 The old Church School
The Thundersley National School began its life in 1856, and rather like Hadleigh's National School, built a year earlier, it had been intended, hoped for and expected for a good number of years. In the distance on the right is the weather-boarded cottage that still stands almost opposite Raymonds Drive.

93 Thundersley Church School, postmarked 1906
Date stamped "Rayleigh 1906 May 17th 1.45pm", the reverse of the card explains that the sender would like to be met at Kentish Town Station at around 8 o'clock the following evening.

94 Thundersley Church School, postmarked 1908
When the new state school was built in Dark Lane in 1921 the old school (pictured here) continued for a further seven years before entirely giving up its original purpose. During the 1960s the building was used for the Thundersley Public Lending Library.

95 Junction Church Road and Kenneth Road, postmarked 1909
We are standing at Pond's Corner where Kenneth Road now meets Hart Road, looking east towards the village centre. The four houses on the immediate left, once known as Raymonds Terrace, are still there and previously belonged to Raymonds Farm and originally would have housed agricultural labourers.

96 Church Road (now Hart Road) (reproduced from glass negative)
The first telegraph pole on the left indicates where Raymond's Drive turns off to the left. The two cottages in the splendid old weather-boarded house on the right are still with us. One is named Rose Cottage and the other in 1955 was known mysteriously as Enigma.

97 Church Road (now Hart Road)
This shop we have seen before in 11, 95 and 96. Currently it is a barber's. Many readers will remember the Cutley Lynch pub which stood next door, now replaced by Castle Point Gas & Heating.

98 Hart Cottages
We have arrived back in the centre of the village with views of Hart Cottages, The White Hart and, in the far distance, Strathmore, standing at the start of Common Approach and the beginning of Tour Two.

TOUR TWO

TOUR TWO begins once again at the White Hart. Our walk is much shorter than Tour One and it is also free of steep hills. From the hostelry we head north towards Thundersley Great Common. En route we pause at the junction of Hart Road and Common Approach and then, as the Common comes into view, we pass old Cedar Hall Farm, formerly known as Sayers Farm. Once upon the Great Common it is tempting to follow some of the lanes and footpaths. A short walk down Great Burches Road brings us to Little Common and a wonderful long view from Crossfell Road. The Great Common itself has much to recommend it as a place for leisurely strolls and quiet picnics but we can also admire some of the flora that naturally inhabit this place.

We follow the main footpath across the Common and after a while bear east to find ourselves in Kingsley Lane where a handful of new bungalows has been built. At the lane's end we turn left in Rayleigh Road to briefly admire the new Arterial Road from London with its great roundabout beside the Weir Hotel. Retracing our steps we head south on Rayleigh Road where we discover an ever increasing number of shops, mostly on the right hand side. These include a post office, a corn merchant's and several general stores. After a short hill the road descends to a crossroads once known locally as the Four Wantz. Just before we reach the junction, to the right is Common Lane which we shall venture into briefly before admiring the flower-growing field behind Kiln Farm Cottages. These cottages, once a farmhouse, face on to Rayleigh Road exactly opposite Daws Heath Road. The dominating building at the Four Wantz is the Woodmans Arms, a public house which has stood here for many a year refreshing the weary traveller and the locals.

Now we walk westwards along Hart Road heading for Swans Green where we leave the road, taking the locals' much preferred route to the village centre across the Green and through the gate into Dark Lane. We will see Thundersley School (built 1921) on our left before we let ourselves out by another gate close to Hart Cottages and then return to the White Hart.

99 The White Hart Pub
This is a very early postcard which reveals the White Hart in all its former weather-boarded glory. There seems to be plenty of activity around the smithy on the far side of the pub.

100   Hart Road
Here we are at the junction of Hart Road and Common Approach, looking eastwards along the former. Note the hedge and field on the right where now stands a parade of shops with its own access road. Strathmore is just out of vision on the left.

101   Hart Road, postmarked 1952
Standing in Hart Road near Cedar Road (to our right) looking north-west. this view has not changed very much in the last seven decades, although a cluster of town houses has just been built to the left of our view point.

102 Strathmore, Common Approach
Strathmore, the house behind the signpost, was destroyed by a bomb on 24th November 1940, killing the occupants, Rebecca and Ellen Harvey and their nephew, Stanley, who had just popped in to see his aunts shortly after visiting his wife's grave at St Peter's. The house was rebuilt and is there today.

103 Sayers Farm, alias Cedar Hall
Better known as Cedar Hall Farm these premises stood facing Thundersley Common on the corner of Common Approach opposite Burches Road. Cedar Hall was a nineteenth century change of name. For centuries it was a 200 acre farm known as Sayers.

104 Cedar Hall Farm in the snow
The deep snow in the southern extent of the Great Common helps to show off the magnificent spread of the Cedar of Lebanon standing behind the farmhouse. It also enables us to see more sharply the various barns and outbuildings belonging to the farm.

105 Panorama – Thundersley plotland cottages circa 1905
Spring Cottage, in the foreground of this view of Great Burches Road, looks far from spring-like in this wintry view. Both buildings shown were early plotland cottages, the farther one being Braeside. Both these sites have been redeveloped.

106 View from Thundersley Common
From Little Common we are looking down Crossfell Road then a remarkably wide "green lane". It drops down steeply to the west with (once upon a time) an uninterrupted view for many miles. The lack of visible plotland cottages suggest this is an early postcard.

107 View of Thundersley Common
This attractive postcard was posted in Hadleigh in 1911. As the only substantial road leading from the Common this is likely to be Great Burches Road. Note the piles of shingles beside the road, presumably to help repair potholes.

108 Thundersley Common
We are looking south and Cedar Hall is now partially hidden by bushes and in some state of disrepair. The photographer is standing in the road called The Common. Great Burches Road can be seen heading off to the right.

109 Thundersley Common
The photographer employed here has created a great sense of large open space. In the middle ground on the right a group of people, perhaps a family, are sitting on the grass, enjoying the Common and perhaps the weather.

110 Thundersley Great Common, postmarked 1928
Before the coming of the A127 Arterial Road, the track passing across the Common connected with a footpath at the northern end of the Common and once made a very good route for locals to visit Rayleigh without first trekking east to the Rayleigh Road. Siluria and Dewsland, the large semi-detached pair on the right, still stand.

111 View of Thundersley Common, circa 1916
The Great Common displays luxuriant plant growth. Some of the plants on view are believed to be Soft Rush, Tufted Hair-grass, Heather, Bracken and Gorse, all of which are typical of acidic heathland and have all been recorded regularly on the Common over the years.

112 Funeral, Kingsley Lane
This would appear to be a child's funeral in 1909 conducted by the Peculiar People, several of whom lived in Kingsley Lane at the time. The semi-detached bungalows were some of the first houses in the lane and still survive today although with a variety of alterations.

113 Weir Corner, Rayleigh
Bliss for car drivers at the almost empty Weir roundabout shortly after World War Two. The view is from Thundersley looking across the Southend Arterial Road to Rayleigh and a perfectly recognisable Weir public house.

114 Rayleigh Road, Thundersley (just south of Hacks Drive)
Clifford Brigham, a Norfolk soldier of the 1st London Divisional Engineers was billeted at the house marked with the cross on May 18th 1916, when he wrote home to his mother, residing at Lyng near Norwich, requesting his plimsols to be sent. In August he was posted to France but survived the ordeal. The house, Silverleigh, also survives.

115 Rayleigh Road
From close to Deerhurst we are looking towards the Weir. The house on the right is still there and the field beyond remains a field in 2019, but for how much longer with the council under pressure to build more houses? The fire station now occupies the middle distance. Holy Trinity Church, Rayleigh, can just be made out on the skyline.

116 Rayleigh Road
Our view is still towards the Weir but from a greater distance. The three large houses with identical design spaced down the right hand side of the road are still there. The furthest one is the house in the previous postcard, 115.

117 Lois Wiggins with billeting soldiers WW1
During the 1st World War, Lois had to temporarily billet soldiers in her family home on the north corner of Deerhurst. The irony of the situation was that the Wiggins family were members of the Peculiar People and objected to fighting in the war. Lois's husband, Stan, was imprisoned in Dartmoor as a conscientious objector, sentenced to hard labour.

118 The Kings Royal Rifles, Rayleigh Road
The Kings Royal Rifles were also billeted locally during the 1st World War. There exists a companion postcard which shows the same regiment marching along Hadleigh High Street. The house with the flagpole in the front garden was probably being used by officers as a temporary HQ.

119 Thundersley Post Office
On the left is Mount Pleasant in Rayleigh Road which was purpose built as home and post office in 1911 by the Sub-Postmaster, Frederick W. Harrod. He had run the previous post office in a smaller house just off picture to the left of Mount Pleasant.

120 Thundersley Post Office

We are at the top of the rise in Rayleigh Road, just past The Woodman's Arms. First on the left is what became Keys' Stores and had once been a post office. Next door to it is Mount Pleasant, the post office referred to in the title. It is now a private house.

121 Fred Harrod's Christmas Card, 1926

It was once not unusual for Christmas Greetings to be sent by postcard. Fred Harrod, the enterprising postmaster at Mount Pleasant, produced his own postcards of local views, several of which appear in this volume. His father was bishop to the Peculiar People at Daws Heath and Fred was one of his assistants.

122 Keys' hay cart
Sid Keys ran a sizeable business in corn and coal. He was able to buy land behind his shop for his yard which extended down to Common Lane. After Sid's death, Wiggins bought the land and developed a road of houses off Common Lane called Keysland, in honour of Sid.

123 Sid Keys, Corn Merchant
This postcard was sent by Mr Hawkins from Mount Pleasant in Rayleigh. He was apparently running short of chicken feed. By curious coincidence Keys' shop and yard stood in Rayleigh Road next to Thundersley`s Mount Pleasant.

124 **Olive Keys and the Keys' shop, Rayleigh Road.**
This one-time post office, now Benfleet Physiotherapy, became the centre of the business of the Keys family. Standing in the doorway is Olive Keys, one of the younger children of Sid and Ellen Keys.

125 **Grigg's Shop, circa 1912**
The very large Thundersley Grigg family were mainly to be found at Daws Heath where they were members of the Peculiar People. They pursued a variety of occupations including shopkeeping. This business, a lean-to against their house at 3 Hillside, Rayleigh Road, is just one of three known Grigg shops.

126 High Road at Common Lane, Thundersley (reproduced from glass negative)
Standing by Common Lane we look up the hill towards Rayleigh. The last house on the left is Mount Pleasant – see postcard 119. An interesting long lost shop called The Little Women is the first on the left and although this scene is pre-World War II, the shop was still active in 1956.

127 High Road at Common Lane, Thundersley
The camera is pointing up Rayleigh Road from the corner of Common Lane. Most of the buildings shown are still standing today. The first house, on the corner, is semi-detached and was for many years occupied by the Fuller family who ran the High Road Stores, the tall building to the left of the telegraph pole.

128 Common Lane
In the distance the keen-eyed will be able to spot the Woodmans Arms. The weather-boarded house, Rose Villa, still stands prominently in Common Lane although its wooden surround has gone.

129 Ed Fuller, flower grower
When he retired from the police force, Ed Fuller ran a flower growing business. Apart from his garden he also used this piece of land between Common Lane and Hart Road, behind where the row of shops now stands on Rayleigh Road. In the distance is a gate leading on to Common Lane with Edward`s house on its corner.

130 Kiln Farm Cottages
Once known as Kiln Farm these cottages stood facing The Woodmans. They were rented by Joe Wiggins from 1880. His son, Stan, bought the building, his birthplace, and its 12 acres of farmland on both sides of the Rayleigh Road for £12,000 in 1919. Demolished 1927 and replaced by a row of shops.

131 The Woodmans Arms
In Rayleigh Road a uniformed postman, only a short distance from his place of employment, stands in front of a very traditional Essex weather-boarded public house, the Woodmans Arms. Perhaps he is waiting for the pub to open.

132 The Woodmans Arms
The appearance of the Woodmans here in the first decade of the 20th century had probably changed little since Zachariah Wiltshire was the beer seller in 1851. Zach's fame was assured when a new Thundersley pub, the Zach Willsher, opened in Church Road, New Thundersley in 1979.

133 Woodmans Arms
Before the 1st World War the weather boarding disappeared and was replaced by brick but for some years the further end of the old wooden pub remained as a small house. Front right there is a little triangle of grass at the junction with Daws Heath Road.

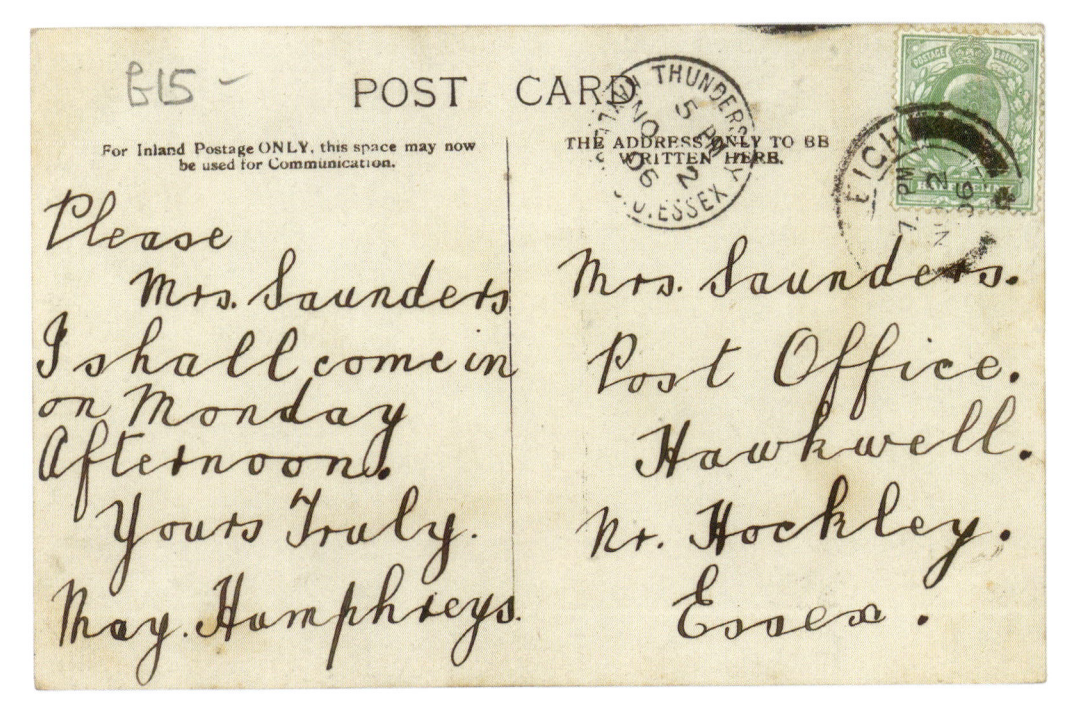

134 The back of post card 132, postmarked 1906
May Humphreys, the sender, was the telegraphist at Mount Pleasant, the Rayleigh Road Post Office, and was boarding in 1911 with sub-postmaster Fred Harrod and his wife, Emma. Miss Humphreys, born in Eastwood, was 13 when she wrote this card in 1906 and perhaps was already working part-time at Hawkwell Post Office.

135 Woodmans Arms (reproduced from glass negative)
An attachment to the pub sign says "PHONE HERE" indicating that a public telephone was available within the pub's premises. If we compare this card with postcard 133, several changes are evident. A porch now protects the new bay window of the Saloon Bar and a third entrance has replaced a window at the nearer end of the pub.

TDSY.19 WOODMANS CORNER, THUNDERSLEY Copyright Frith's.

136 Woodmans Corner
Later than postcard 135, this card reveals a few changes to the façade of the Woodman, the wooden building and the water trough have disappeared and a kerb has appeared. Rayleigh Road was once a popular shopping area and several of the shops can be seen on the left including High Road Stores, later Hillside Stores, with the nearer sunblind.

137 Prize-giving at The Woodman's
A country run has taken place and Mrs Potter the "Woodmans' licensee" is handing out the prizes to the first three past the tape, listed on the little blackboard as Bardell G., Marshall G. and Baber W.H.. Presumably the mantlepiece clock acted as a timer and Mr Bardell took 19 minutes to win.

138 Orchard Villas
This pair of semi-detached houses still stands on the left, just before the townhouses and Cedar Hall School, as you travel eastwards on Hart Road. The appearance of the building has changed considerably especially in the case of the left hand house.

139 Hart Road Caravan Site
This caravan site between Cedar Hall School and Swans Green looks very different now with its static vans, much tidier although more densely populated, but it has been a feature of Hart Road for more than half a century.

140 Swans Green

A narrow Hart Road with encroaching bushes leads us westwards towards Swans Green which once was known as Goose Green. This is one of Fred Harrod's postcards.

141 Swans Green

The grassy track going off to the left, still popular with pedestrians, nowadays has a hard surface. It runs across the Green to the trees where it becomes Dark Lane, passing Thundersley Primary School and emerging in the heart of the village.

142 Swans Green
From the southern side of Swans Green we are able to see Hart Road before a hedgeline interrupted the view. The house in front of the elms is Swan Cottage which once had been one of two small workhouses admitting poor people from both Thundersley and South Benfleet. *[See article The Thundersley Workhouse in www.hadleighhistory.org.uk]*

143 Dark Lane
We are standing in Dark Lane looking back to Swans Green which is beyond the white gate. At one time there was a gate at each end of the lane.

144 Thundersley Schools
The school was opened in 1921 and is now called Thundersley Primary School.

145 Dark Lane
This fence and gate once stood at the western end of Dark Lane. The school would later be built beyond the hedge to the right. Just out of sight to the immediate left stood Hart Cottages. *[See also postcards 4, 5 and 6]*

TOUR THREE

TOUR THREE is a very simple walk (2 miles) almost entirely consisting of two roads: Rayleigh Road and Kiln Road, so there is little chance of becoming lost. We head south from the Four Wantz following the Rayleigh Road and almost immediately we will be surprised by a rather lovely duckpond on our left. Soon after that we will spot, also on our left, Balmerino Avenue with its bungalows. There are a number of older houses to be observed mainly on the right of the main road and a well established funeral director's business on both sides of a bend in the road. Soon we will find ourselves approaching Victoria House Corner where three parishes meet, Hadleigh, South Benfleet and Thundersley. We now turn right and venture along Kiln Road, named after the brick kilns which stood here long ago.

There are plenty of houses and businesses on Kiln Road, including a post office, which are worthy of our interest. When we reach Runnymede Chase on our right we will take a diversion on to The Chase in order to take note of one of the entrance gates into Thundersley Lodge, once an estate of considerable importance. Back on Kiln Road we take another diversion, this time to the left into Thundersley Glen with its pond and grand views. Finally we halt this tour at the top of Bread and Cheese Hill having spotted a couple of interesting houses amongst the luxuriant roadside bush growth.

146 The Woodmans Arms

Here we are back at the Four Wantz about to take the Rayleigh Road towards Hadleigh. This is a further view of the Woodmans Arms as it was in the first decade of the 20th century. Spot the horse's head!

147 Woodmans Arms junction
This is one of the most startling postcards in this collection. The quiet country crossroads once known as the Four Wantz is now an incredibly busy junction with two mini-roundabouts. To the left is Daws Heath Road with Hart Road to the right. The tree-lined country lane straight ahead is the Rayleigh Road heading south towards Hadleigh.

148 Rayleigh Road
Only a short distance down the road from the Wantz and looking back over our shoulders we can see the peaceful and remarkably spacious junction from yet another viewpoint.

149 Duck pond, junction Rayleigh Road and Daws Heath Road
A rare postcard reveals the long forgotten and rather splendid duck pond on the south east corner of the Four Wantz, and once part of Kiln Farm. In the background we can see Daws Heath Road and the cottages seen later in postcard 176.

150 Balmerino Avenue, postmarked 1929
Posted 4th July 1929 the postcard shows Balmerino Avenue in its early days. Elsie, the sender of the card is holidaying in the first bungalow on the left, with her baby. The Avenue dates from 1923.

151 Rayleigh Road (formerly Hadleigh Road)
Balmerino is yet to be built in the distance on the right as we look back towards the Woodmans. The nearest house is still there and used to have Boosey's Coalyard as its north side neighbour. A small amount of the interesting iron work, immediately to the left, remains to this day in front of a house which is just out of sight on this card.

152 Rayleigh Road (formerly Hadleigh Road)
In 1915 Archibald R. Adams expanded his funeral business in Poplar to Thundersley and later to Rayleigh. The firm's business continues today in the same buildings on the right hand side of the bend.. At the time of this postcard it also had premises on the left.

153 Hadleigh Road (now Rayleigh Road)
It will seem almost unbelievable to today's car drivers to see Rayleigh Road so empty and rural. Adams premises are the buildings on the horizon to the left of the road. Today Virgin Active stands opposite Adams.

154 Rayleigh Road A129
Here we are approaching Victoria House Corner. On the left a sign points down Arcadian Gardens to the Hadleigh Baptist Church (founded 1926). It would appear that pavements may soon grace Rayleigh Road judging by the kerb stones heaped on the right hand verge.

155 Rayleigh Road, postmarked 1906 or 1909 (smudged)
This house which still stands close to Kiln Road was built in 1900 as a wedding gift to Dr. Cosmo Grant from his father-in-law, William Sheridan. The former was the first resident doctor in either Thundersley or Hadleigh. The latter, a wealthy industrialist, was involved heavily in the social and political life of the two villages and was a generous philanthropist.

156 Victoria House Corner
We have reached Victoria House Corner which has acquired electric street lamps. The old lodge for Victoria House which showed in postcard 154 has been demolished and several major changes to the properties have taken place if we compare the two cards.

157 Kiln Road (reproduced from glass negative)
Standing where Pendlestone is now, the photographer has caught a number of now lost houses on the south side of the road. The Gospel Hall (on the left) is still there but Edgemount, Greywalls, Restormel, West Cottage and Valcastra were demolished (prior to 1995) and replaced by the back gardens of Five Oaks.

158 Kiln Road
This is a similar view to 157, taken after the grass verge had been sacrificed to some road-widening. The houses we are looking at are at the right hand end of the row in the previous postcard. The telegraph poles are a very useful guide. In the distance we can see Parkstone Stores *[see 159]*.

159 Kiln Road, looking west (reproduced from glass negative)
In the middle ground behind the first telegraph pole stands Parkstone Stores with a large Cadbury's advertising board facing the traffic. Standing on the corner of Parkstone Avenue, although now a private dwelling rather than a busy shop, the building is still something of a landmark.

160 Kiln Road, postmarked 1910
The camera is looking east. The first house on the left became Mummery's, now demolished along with its nursery. The next house was Rose Villa, also demolished, whose end wall in later years was painted over, hiding the horizontal striping. Rose Villa stood more or less opposite Parkstone Avenue.

161 Kiln Road Post Office
This quiet little Edwardian scene in front of the post office is in marked contrast to the constant rush of Kiln Road today. Of particular interest is the gap between the two buildings which were later joined together. Both buildings are now private houses and stand quite prominently, east of Badger Hall Avenue.

162 Kiln Road (reproduced from glass negative)
The first house on the left was once called The Warren but today goes under the name of Kiln Lodge and stands on the eastern corner of Warren Chase. In the distance on the right partially hidden by poplars are the pair of houses the farther of which was once the Kiln Road Post Office.

163 Kiln Road (reproduced from glass negative)
Nowadays the nearest building, then Hannaford's Stores, has no chimney and is surrounded by the flat roofed showroom of Fireplace Design Ltd. on the corner of Hermitage Avenue. On the other corner the house has been changed considerably and is now occupied by the Kiln Road Co-op.

164 Kiln Road (reproduced from glass negative)
An earlier picture of the same shop, the wavy-topped "burr" wall has yet to be built (made out of cheap casing bricks, no doubt from one of the local kilns). The clearly flourishing shop was run for many years by its proprietor, Mrs Nellie Hannaford.

165 Kiln Road, postmarked 1914
This cottage has long gone but it stood quite close to what is now the Castle Point Council Offices but on the opposite side of Kiln Road. The postcard was sent from The Retreat Refreshment Rooms, located much nearer Bread & Cheese Hill. *[See 20]*

166 The Chase
Leaving Kiln Road we turn up Runnymede Chase to The Chase. Here we have a view looking eastward and on the right a large gate with pillars can be discerned. This is one entrance to Thundersley Lodge, at one time a 360 acre farm and anciently the Royal Park of Thundersley.

167 Thundersley House, Kiln Road, postmarked 1914
Frank Newman built a number of new houses on the south side of Kiln Road between Thundersley Glen, which he owned, and Badger Hall. One of the earliest was Thundersley House, standing on the left of the entrance to the Glen which provided the clay for the bricks. The Newman family moved into the house in 1923.

168 Thundersley Glen
The Glen, one of Castle Point's most delightful open spaces, was given to the Council by Frank and Mabel Newman. It was the latter who particularly enjoyed the Glen and encouraged young campers, becoming a sort of surrogate "auntie" to some of the trainee teachers who camped there. *[See 168]*

169 Thundersley Glen Pond
When it was privately owned the Glen was very popular with campers on the site near the pond. Shoreditch Training College, for instance, held their annual summer camp here before and after the 1st World War. The pond where they used to swim and boat was filled in during a more litigious age, for health and safety reasons.

170 View to the south from Thundersley Glen
This rather splendid landscape photograph appears to be more of a view from the Glen than the Glen itself. On the left horizon can be seen the South Benfleet Water Tower. Boyce Hill Golf Course is clearly seen on the right.

171 Kiln Road, postmarked 1913
This photograph was taken before the 1st World War and is thought to show the road approaching Bread and Cheese Hill. The white fence on the right is about where the road Konnybrook is situated and may have been the fence surrounding Chelsea House, a substantial dwelling which later became the Council Depot.

172 View near Bread & Cheese Hill
In the distance a bus is passing Kenneth Road and about to descend the hill. Sharp eyes or use of a magnifying glass may espy on the immediate left an advert for Nut Brown tobacco telling us a shop is just off picture. It would be one of ten houses built here in a row during the 1920s and 1930s and still there today.

173 Bread & Cheese Hill
Our third tour ends at the famous hill, conveniently just past the eponymous public house. Once again in the picture we have the shop/café at the corner of Thundersley Park Road which is still remembered by many as Jordan's Store. Across the road is the house at the edge of Coombe Wood. *[see postcard 25]*

174 Near Bread & Cheese Hill
The absence of any obvious landmark makes this picture tricky to locate. Our instinct is that it is taken from a spot just a little downhill from the previous postcard *[173]* a few paces beyond the first telegraph pole. Nowadays this track would barely pass muster as a country lane. The provision of a pavement would one day involve considerable excavation.

TOUR FOUR

TOUR FOUR is into Daws Heath, the Thundersley hamlet, which occupies the eastern end of the parish. Almost immediately as we walk along the Daws Heath Road from the Woodmans Arms we spot on the right the cosy little tollhouse, a remnant of the days when to travel in a vehicle on the main roads was not free. A little further up the slope on the left are a couple of slightly unusual single floor dwellings. They are definitely not in the popular bungalow style. Once we have conquered the gentle slope to its top we are met with a splendid view towards the centre of the hamlet and on our immediate right is the remarkably named Oo Oo Cottage. We pass the third Peculiar People's Chapel on the left. It does not take long to reach the junction with (what is now) Western Road, which heads off to Hadleigh. Here, on the south side, there is a large pond which demonstrates how Great Wyburns once farmed the land on both sides of Daws Heath Road.

We next venture halfway down Western Road to a footpath which leads off to our left. Along here we find the graveyard of the Peculiar People lying behind their second chapel. The Daws Heath Road and Western Road form a triangle which has become the centre of the hamlet. This triangle is seen most clearly when we look northwards at the bottom of Western Road.

Back at the top of Western Road we proceed eastwards following Daws Heath Road. A short distance along the road there is a general store, one of a few business premises in this part of Thundersley. When Daws Heath Road turns off to the south we continue our walk, now along Bramble Road through a mainly rural area. We eventually come to the end of the road where we see a small group of houses clustered in this rather remote place. A turn to the right is made at this point and then a turn to the left into the eastern end of Poors Lane where we may view a very large mansion called Wittering Court. As Tour Four comes to an end, we return the way we came but take a gentle stroll in Pound Wood, one of several wonderful woodlands which can be accessed from Daws Heath.

175 Turnpike Cottage, Daws Heath Road
Setting off once again from the Four Wantz, this time to Daws Heath, on our right is the old tollhouse which was demolished in 1966. When carters deliberately avoided the toll at Victoria House Corner by travelling through Daws Heath an additional tollhouse was created to catch them out.

176 Daws Heath Road
Here we are at the western end of the long road, looking up the hill from the tollhouse. The two nearest and slightly unusual cottages were built by Joseph Wiggins in 1907 on land he had recently puchased. They are still there although with somewhat refurbished exteriors. *[See also postcard 149]*

177 Daws Heath Road, looking west
The camera stands beside what is now the entrance to Deanes School and is looking towards Daws Heath. On the right is Hilltop Cottage (once Oo Oo Cottage) which is still there today. The card is one of many local views by an unknown photographer which enterprising postmaster, Fred Harrod, published and sold.

178 Daws Heath
We look east along a Daws Heath Road which is straighter now. In the middle on the left of the road is Valley Cottage. In the distance we can see a house and just beyond it sticking out behind the house is the third chapel of the Daws Heath Peculiar People built 1894. Both buildings survive.

179 Daws Heath pond
The pond, once part of Great Wyburns farmyard, stood at Clark's Corner on the south side of Daws Heath Road just where Western Road begins. The house in Western Road, behind the pond, was called Ingleside and was once the home of the Adams family. The two young men in the cart are Arthur Rolph and Albert Spicer.

180 Great Wyburns Farm, Daws Heath
We are at what was previously known as Clark's Corner looking towards the west in about 1912. On the right is Great Wyburns, once a 200 acre farm speading across both sides of the Daws Heath Road and the A127. The farmhouse and its numerous outbuildings are long gone.

181 The Peculiar People's graveyard
We are standing on the footpath that links Western Road and Daws Heath Road, facing the latter. The graves are out of sight on the left of the graveyard's path but it is now full. The rather grand mock Tudor house in Daws Heath Road has the surprisingly homely name of Walnut Tree Cottage.

182 Western Road and Daws Heath Road
As we approach the centre of Daws Heath from Hadleigh we reach this fork with Western Road to the left and Daws Heath Road to the right. In the 18th century these two roads were merely a pair of simple footpaths across empty heathland.

183 Daws Heath Road
The semi-detached pair of houses on the right are still there today, standing on the western corner of Sherry Way. The left hand house was once a general stores. The storekeepers down the years included the Thoringtons and the Fullers.

184 Jollity at Daws Heath
Probably not published commercially as a postcard but printed at this popular size in about 1953, so the occasion may have been to do with the Queen's coronation. It is a wonderfully happy picture of residents of Daws Heath. We lack the room to print the names here but an article, Jollity at Daws Heath, with names, has been published on the Archive website.

185 Bramble Road, Daws Heath
The photographer is standing in the middle of Bramble Road at the junction with St Michael's Road. The neatly trimmed hedges belong to a house called Woodlands built by James Mitchell, a Limehouse draper, for his family in the late 1880s. He was probably Daws Heath's first London commuter.

186 Dawes Heath
This view from close to the eastern end of Bramble Road but looking westwards does not appear much different today. The road is still narrow and the houses on the right are still with us. With regard to the postcard's title, the confusion over whether to add an "e" to Daws is several centuries old.

187 Wittering Court
The Edwardian building seen here was replaced after a fire in 2008. It had been a peaceful private residence for nearly ninety years but before that it was a "home for imbeciles and epileptics". The appalling treatment of the inmates led to a trial of the owner's attorney, a verdict of guilty, and the subsequent closure of the home in 1919.

188 In the Woods, circa 1937
The following woods still survive in Thundersley: Pound, Tile, Wyburns, Starvelarks, Valerie Wells, Ragwood, Coombe and North Benfleet Hall. It is not possible to tell which one is depicted here. Thundersley once had even more woods but despite 20th and 21st century threats the above are still with us.

189 Hadleigh & Thundersley Cricket Club, 1946
This team was fielded in the first year of the club's existence. For names of players please refer to the article about this photo on the Archive website. Until 1946 Hadleigh CC and Thundersley CC had led separate lives for perhaps 120 years or more. The Club's website has many photos and names: *www.hadleighandthundersleycricketclub.co.uk/heritage*.

YOUR OWN LOCAL HISTORY

If you have enjoyed the postcards and wish to further your knowledge of any of the places, people or related events you may well find more information in the book "Thundersley & Daws Heath – A History" by Robert Hallmann (which has a useful index). Robert's magnificent book, published by the Hadleigh & Thundersley Community Archive, is full of detail and stories of Thundersley.

Another source of further information is the H&TCA website: www.hadleighhistory.org.uk The site has a search button for those seeking more information.

If you would like to comment on any of the postcards, perhaps to tell us your memories of places, people or events, please use the website. Your reflections would be welcome. If you have strong memories why not write a short piece for the website? Just click on "Add Article" and follow the instructions.

AN ARMCHAIR TOUR

The following postcards do not fit comfortably into our four tours but nevertheless we felt they deserved a fresh airing. The first five are all multi-view cards, or "Peeps", as they came to be known. (There's one more on page 9.) These were good sellers. With up to five views and a cheery salutation on each, perhaps folk felt they were getting more for their money? Or, it may have simply been that they didn't have to deliberate too long as to which scene their recipient would prefer – with a Peeps postcard they could simply "hedge their bet". In a way, these Peeps postcards offer a mini-tour each.

Where a view on the next five postcards is identical to one of those on the "Tours", the number of the postcard is given in square brackets.

190 Peeps, postmarked 1943
Top: Thundersley Common *[110]*; Thundersley Schools
Middle: St Peter's *[70]*
Bottom: Thundersley Post Office *[119]*; Southend Road Thundersley (Woodmans Arms)

191 Peeps, postmarked 1920
Top: Kenneth Road; Bird's Eye View *[67]*
Middle: View by Church
Bottom: The Pond, Great Tarpots; View Thundersley Common *[111]*

192 Peeps
Top: Thundersley Common; Thundersley Church (Interior)
Middle: Kiln Farm Duck Pond *[149]*
Bottom: Thundersley Church (Lych Gate); Church & Rectory, Thundersley *[72]*

193 Peeps, postmarked 1910
   Published by Geo. W. Hand of Thundersley *[see 89]* but printed in Germany.
   Top: Hart Pond (and Cottages); The (Church) School *[94]*
   Middle: The Parish Church (St Peter's)
   Bottom: Interior Thundersley Church; Raymonds Farm *[9]*

194 Peeps, postmarked 1908
   Top: Thundersley Church; Thundersley (Church) School *[94]*
   Bottom: Raymonds Farm *[9]*; Hart Pond (and Cottages); Thundersley (White Hart)

195 View from the Devil's Steps, postmarked 1961
Whilst the Devil's Steps are firmly in the parish of South Benfleet, they would have been familiar to the majority of Thundersleyites as they were the steepest part of the most direct pedestrian route to South Benfleet (via Boyce Hill). The path is still walkable, apart from the very top bit by Thundersley Park Road, which has been lost under development.

196 Wild Card – a Thundersley Barn, but where?
This card was never posted, but is inscribed with dip pen and sepia ink, *"Summer 1908"* Circumstantial evidence implies that it is indeed Thundersley, but its location is an unsolved mystery. The restoration from faded original revealed a baby perched precariously atop the cart – it's likely the mother had forty fits when she saw the postcard in her local Post Office!

197 Thundersley Band
The location is most likely to be somewhere in South Benfleet but the band is definitely the Thundersley Band, sufficiently established at this time to have their name emblazoned on the bass drum. Claude "Stan" Wiggins (b. 1882) founding father of the Wiggins Builders empire, is on clarinet. This postcard is not postmarked but is likely to be from a little before 1914.

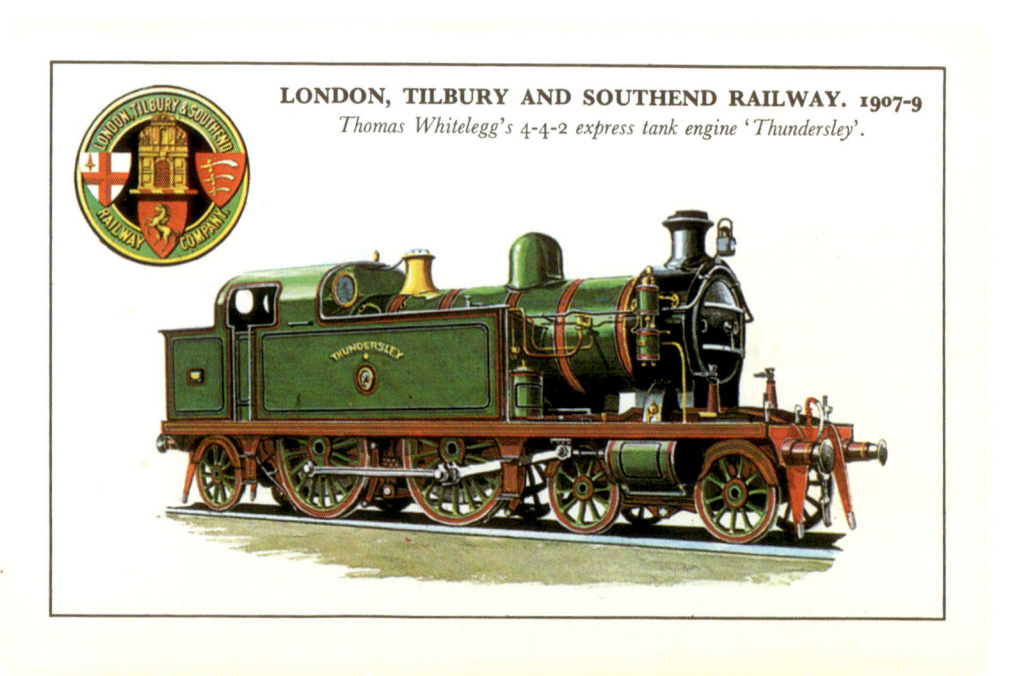

198 LT&SR tank engine, Thundersley
This card is one of a large series published by Colourmaster Photo Precision. In 1909, the London, Tilbury & Southend Railway ordered four 79 Class 4-4-2T suburban tank engines, designed by Whitelegg and built by Robert Stephenson & Co. at Derby. No 80 "Thundersley" was decommissioned in 1956 but survives at Bressingham Steam Museum.

199 Thundersley Park Road, Jarvis Hill, postmarked 1916
Strictly speaking, the location here is South Benfleet, not Thundersley. In the early 20th Century this new road afforded a shorter route linking the two localities, avoiding the ancient but steeper and more treacherous path through Jarvis Wood (the Glen).

200 View from Benfleet Hill towards Thundersley, postmarked 1917
Here the A13 London Road runs east west along a high ridge (around the 75m contour), with Thundersley to the north and South Benfleet and the River Thames to the south. The topography is challenging, but the smattering of dwellings are probably near Thundersley Park Road. Note the elm trees, once ubiquitous but now a fading memory.

A brief history of postcards in Britain and clues to identifying their age

Postcards were first introduced in Britain by the Post Office in 1870. These early postcards bore an embossed ½d stamp and were thinner and smaller than the present-day type. The address appeared one side and the message on the other. No charge was made by the Post Office for the postcard itself.

In 1894, after much lobbying from stationers, permission was granted for the use of commercially produced postcards to which a halfpenny adhesive stamp could be fixed. The age of the Picture Postcard had begun.

From 1899 onwards, the standard size (already in use in other countries) of 3½" by 5½" was accepted in Britain.

However, only the address, and nothing else, could be written on the front of the card. The message went on the back, often sharing the space with a picture.

In 1902 the Post Office led the field, changing its rules to allow a division on the address side, so that the left-hand side could be used for a message. Often a line was printed to mark the division.

A legible postmark clearly establishes the latest possible date of a postcard's production but, of course, the card might have been published many years earlier (or, indeed, the photograph could be from an even earlier date). If the date is not legible, the stamp can be a guide.

The normal (inland) postage rate for postcards remained at ½d for almost fifty years, until 1918.

On 3rd June 1918 the inland rate was doubled to 1d, resulting in a decline in the number of postcards posted. Within three years there was a further increase to 1½d. However, in the wake of much ill-feeling, during May 1922 it was reduced back to a penny.

In 1925 new international sizes for postcards were adopted, being Maximum 5⅞" x 4⅛" Minimum 4" x 2¾"

In May 1940 the postcard rate rose to 2d. There were to be two further increases, to 2½d in 1957 and 3d in 1965, before the Special Rate for Postcards was finally abolished in May 1965.

Postcards can also be roughly dated by the portrait on the stamp. This is not *quite* as easy as it sounds because the sovereign's name does not feature – and both Edward VII (1901–1910) and George V (1910–1936) appear balding and bearded!

In the days before widespread ownership of telephones, postcards were, in effect, "the poor man's telegram". Three postal deliveries a day meant that a sailor could arrive in port early morning and, quite literally, write to his wife that she might expect him home for tea that same day.

Picture postcards were sometimes collected as keepsakes, but more on account of their pictures than their messages: yet few of our ancestors would have imagined that these humble items of ephemera would hold us quite so spellbound a century later!

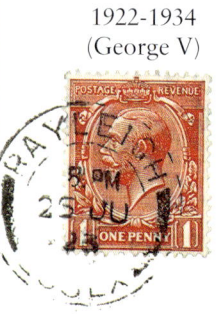